MW00993362

# CHEETAH

## TAYLOR MORRISON

HENRY HOLT AND COMPANY • NEW YORK

<<< ◆ >>>

Author's Note:
Duma, the name of the mother cheetah in this story, is short for "enduma."
This is the Swahili term for cheetah.

Henry Holt and Company, Inc., *Publishers since 1866*, 115 West 18th Street, New York, New York 10011
Henry Holt is a registered trademark of Henry Holt and Company, Inc.

Library of Congress Cataloging-in-Publication Data
Morrison, Taylor.
Cheetah / Taylor Morrison.
Summary: Describes a day in the life of a cheetah family in the Serengeti National Park as the mother hunts
to feed her cubs.
1. Cheetah—Tanzania—Serengeti National Park—Juvenile literature. 2. Serengeti National Park (Tanzania) [1. Cheetah.
2. Serengeti National Park (Tanzania)] I. Title. QL737.C23 M6735 1997 599.75'9—dc21 97-16683

ISBN 0-8050-5121-X First Edition—1998 Printed in the United States of America on acid-free paper ∞
10 9 8 7 6 5 4 3 2 1
The artist used acrylic paint on canvas to create the illustrations for this book.

## To Naomi

Thank you to Dan, Jean, and Barbara for allowing me
to study their beautiful cheetahs at Wildlife Safari
— T. M.

A family of cheetahs rises with the morning sun. It is late May on the long grass plain of Tanzania's Serengeti National Park. The rains have begun to die out as the dry season draws near. High upon a termite mound, a mother cheetah, Duma, watches thousands of wildebeest grazing in the vast ocean of grass. Her cubs, only three months old, are completely dependent on Duma to feed them.

In the cool morning air, the brothers are playing. They take turns chasing and knocking each other down. This game develops their hunting reflexes. By becoming good hunters, the cheetahs will help to control the population of herd animals.

As she walks into the grass, the cubs eagerly follow the bouncing white tip of Duma's tail. With a soft, quiet yelp, she tells her cubs to wait. The young cheetahs lie still while their mother hunts. They watch for lions or hyenas, who often eat cheetah cubs.

Duma glides, as smooth as a shadow, through the grass. The coarse yellow fur and soft black spots of her coat and the long black tear marks on her face help to hide her from the wildebeest. The cheetah waits, listening to the honks and grunts coming from the herd. With luck, a surprise attack will scare the powerful adults away from the smaller calves.

Suddenly Duma explodes into a sprint toward the wildebeest and the herd scatters frantically. In the confusing crowd of pounding hooves, Duma catches a young calf and brings it down.

But all the commotion has caught the attention of a hungry lioness. The five-hundred-pound cat charges in and takes the meal. At one hundred twenty pounds, Duma is no match for her. Duma slinks away, growling in frustration.

Duma leads her cubs far away from the dangerous lion to a rock formation called a "kopje" (kop-ee). The father of the cubs and his brother watch the family from afar. The cubs sniff the elder cheetahs' urine markings on the rocks.

The scent warns other full-grown male intruders that this territory belongs to someone else. This keeps male cheetahs from hunting the same prey or mating with the same female cheetahs.

The mother cheetah shows her cubs how to find puddles of rainwater on the rocks to drink from. Then the family flops down under the cool shade of an acacia (a-*kay*-see-a) tree for a nap. The cats purr loudly, relieved to have escaped the relentless heat of the midday sun.

After a long rest, Duma begins to survey the plain for prey. With her keen eyesight, she spots a herd of Thomson's gazelles. Slowly she climbs down from the rocks. She knows she must complete her hunt before the sun goes down. Like all cheetahs, her vision is poor in the dark, and hyenas and lions dominate the night.

Duma's eyes open wide into an intense stare as she begins her stalk. She crouches low, hiding behind a thin screen of swaying grass. She must get close enough to catch a gazelle in a burst of speed, otherwise it will outrun her with its greater endurance.

A gazelle looks up, checking for danger, and Duma freezes. After a few moments, the gazelle's watchful eyes lower again to the grass. An hour passes. But the cheetah never looks away from the nervous gazelles.

A curious giraffe begins to follow Duma. The giraffe stares unafraid and gives the cheetah's position away. The gazelles spread the alarm by snorting, swinging their tails, and stamping their hooves.

Duma's tail swishes in agitation. Her last seven hunting attempts have been failures. The cubs must be fed soon or they will starve.

With a glorious burst of power, Duma's large back leg muscles launch her forward.

The cheetah's spine arches and bends. Taking giant strides, her body is propelled forward. Within two seconds, she is running at forty-five miles per hour. The frantic gazelles bound away at the sight of the yellow blur speeding toward them. One gazelle panics and strays from the safety of the herd.

Duma races after it at seventy miles per hour.

Running in sharp zigzags, the gazelle tries desperately to elude her. But the cheetah keeps up. Her long, flat tail acts as a rudder and a balance to help her make quick turns. Duma's unre-tractable blunt claws grip the ground like cleats on a runner's shoe. But after ten seconds she begins to tire out.

The darting gazelle must be caught now.

Shifting her weight backward, Duma hooks the haunches of the gazelle with her only sharp claw, the dewclaw, and knocks the animal off balance.

As the gazelle tumbles to the ground, Duma lunges for the animal's neck and holds a bite on its throat until it quickly suffocates.

After the exhausting run, Duma's large chest heaves rapidly in and out. Weak with fatigue, she drags the prey under a tree for cover. With high-pitched chirps she calls her hungry cubs. The hairs on their short manes stick up in excitement as they feast. Duma eats after her cubs, pausing frequently to scan the horizon for threatening predators.

The cheetahs leave the gazelle unfinished as haunting cackles fill the night. Hyena clans are heading out to hunt and will soon come to scavenge what is left.

Duma finds a safe patch of grass as the plain sinks into darkness. In the cool night breeze the family huddles together for warmth. Somewhere a lion roars, but the sound is far enough away. The small cubs fall asleep as their mother licks their faces clean.

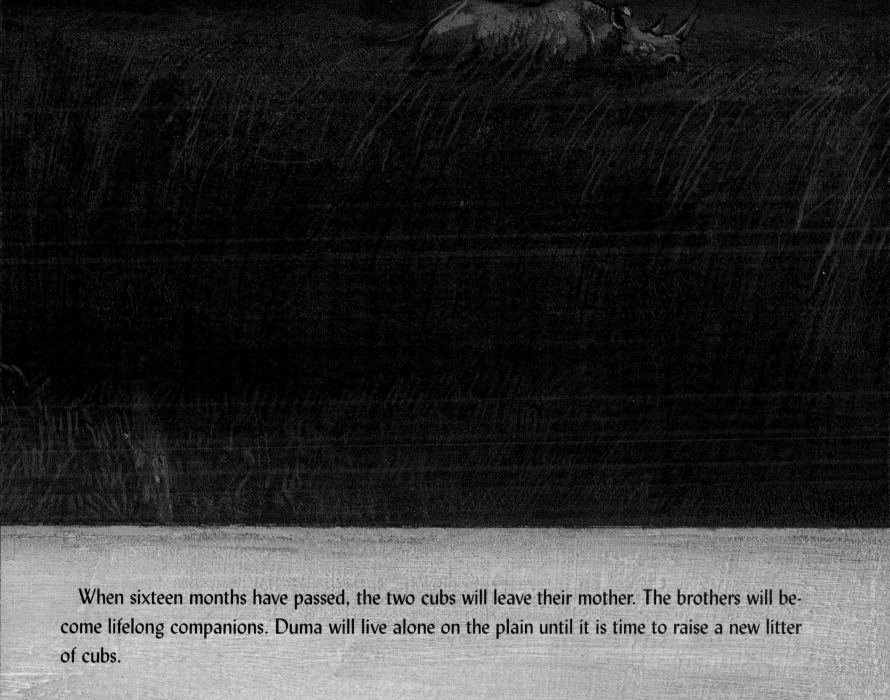

When sixteen months have passed, the two cubs will leave their mother. The brothers will become lifelong companions. Duma will live alone on the plain until it is time to raise a new litter of cubs.

---

---

The fastest animal on land is losing the race against extinction. Not only do cheetahs face competition with predators in the wild, but now they must survive the most dangerous threat of all: humans. As our population grows, so does the need for land and food. But as people take over more and more land for farming, the cheetahs' habitat shrinks. Naturally, this situation creates conflicts as the needs of people and the needs of animals collide.

While the fate of the cheetah may look bleak, there are people fighting to change that. Organizations such as the Cheetah Conservation Fund work to preserve these unique animals in their native home of Africa. And in the United States, there is a lush park in Oregon called Wildlife Safari that offers a safe home for many cheetahs. People visit the park and watch the animals from their cars. With careful monitoring by organizations like these, there is hope that the next generation of cheetahs will survive.

Scientists predict that the cheetah may become extinct within ten to twenty years. But the cheetah's enemy is also the one who can save him. With education and public awareness, this extraordinary animal will continue to thrive for years to come.

---

---